Let's DRAW!

WILD ANIMALS

How2DrawAnimals

Brimming with creative inspiration, how-to projects, and useful information to enrich your everyday life, quarto.com is a favorite destination for those pursuing their interests and passions.

© 2022 Quarto Publishing Group USA Inc.
Illustrations and text © 2022 P. Mendoza

First published in 2022 by Walter Foster Jr., an imprint of The Quarto Group.
100 Cummings Center, Suite 265D, Beverly, MA 01915, USA.
T (978) 282-9590 **F** (978) 283-2742 **www.quarto.com** • **www.walterfoster.com**

Walter Foster Jr. titles are also available at discount for retail, wholesale, promotional, and bulk purchase. For details, contact the Special Sales Manager by email at specialsales@quarto.com or by mail at The Quarto Group, Attn: Special Sales Manager, 100 Cummings Center, Suite 265D, Beverly, MA 01915, USA.

ISBN: 978-0-7603-8076-5

Digital edition published in 2022
eISBN: 978-0-7603-8077-2

Printed in China
10 9 8 7 6 5 4 3

TABLE OF CONTENTS

TOOLS & MATERIALS

Welcome! You don't need much to start learning how to draw. Anyone can draw with just a pencil and piece of scrap paper, but if you want to get more serious about your art, additional artist's supplies are available.

PAPER If you choose printer paper, buy a premium paper that is thick enough and bright. Portable sketch pads keep all your drawings in one place, which is convenient. For more detailed art pieces, use a fine art paper.

PENCILS Standard No. 2 pencils and mechanical pencils are great to start with and inexpensive. Pencils with different graphite grades can be very helpful when shading because a specific grade (such as 4H, 2B, or HB) will only get so dark.

PENCIL SHARPENER Electric sharpeners are faster than manual ones, but they also wear down pencils faster. It's most economical to use an automatic one for inexpensive pencils and a manual sharpener for expensive ones.

ERASERS Some erasers can smear, bend, and even tear your paper, so get a good one that erases cleanly without smudges. Kneaded erasers are pliable and can be molded for precise erasing. They leave no residue, and they last a long time.

PENS If you want to outline a drawing after sketching it, you can use a regular Sharpie® pen or marker. For more intricate pieces, try Micron® pens, which come in a variety of tip thicknesses.

DRAWING BASICS

How to Draw Shapes

For the first steps of each project in this book, you will be drawing basic shapes as guide lines. Use light, smooth strokes and don't press down too hard with your pencil. If you sketch lightly at first, it will be easier to erase if you make a mistake.

You'll be drawing a lot of circles, which many beginning artists find difficult to create. These circles do not have to be perfect because they are just guides, but if you want to practice making better circles, try the four-marks method, as shown below.

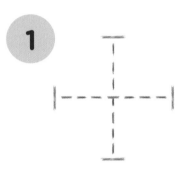

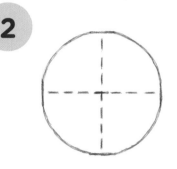

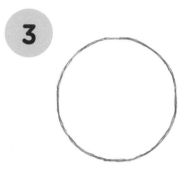

1 Mark where you want the top of the circle and, directly below, make another mark for the bottom. Do the same for the sides of the circle. If it helps, lightly draw a dotted line to help you place the other mark.

2 Once you have the four marks spaced apart equally, connect them using curved lines.

3 Erase any dotted lines you created, and you have a circle!

ADDITIONAL SHAPES While circles are usually what people find the most challenging, there are many other lines and shapes that you should practice and master. An arc can become a muzzle or tongue. Triangles can be ears, teeth, or claws. A football shape can become an eye. A curvy line can make a tail and an angled line a leg. Study the animal and note the shapes that stand out to you.

How to Shade

The final step to drawing an animal is to add shading so that it looks three-dimensional, and then adding texture so that it looks furry, feathery, smooth, or scaly. To introduce yourself to shading, follow the steps below.

1

Understand your pencil with a value scale. Using any pencil, start to shade lightly on one side and gradually darken your strokes toward the other side. This value scale will show you how light and dark your pencil can be.

2

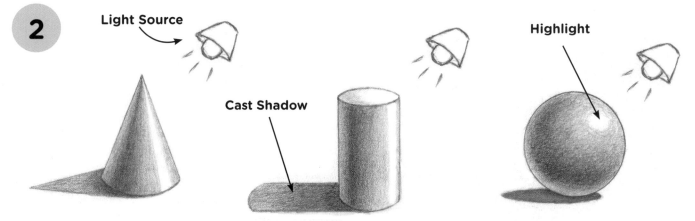

Light Source

Cast Shadow

Highlight

Apply the value scale to simple shapes. Draw simple shapes and shade them to make them look three-dimensional. Observe shadows in real life. Study how the light interacts with simple objects and creates shadows. Then try drawing what you see.

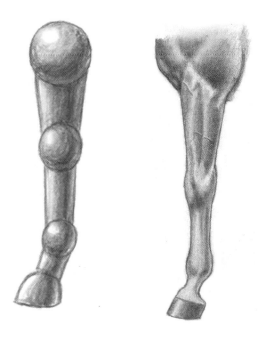

3

Practice with more complex objects. Once you're comfortable shading simple objects, move on to more complex ones. Note, for example, how a horse's leg is made up of cylinders and spheres. Breaking down your subject into simple shapes makes it easier to visualize the shadows.

How to Add Texture

Take what you've learned about shading one step further by adding texture to your drawings.

FURRY

One quick pencil stroke creates a single hair. Keep adding more quick, short strokes and you'll get a furry texture. Separate each individual stroke a bit so that the white of the paper comes through.

Create stripes and patterns by varying the pressure on your pencil to get different degrees of tonal value.

Make sure that your strokes follow the forms of the animal. As you shade a furry animal, use strokes that go in the general direction of the fur growth. The fur here follows the form of a simple sphere.

 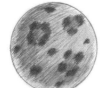

This is how to add fur to a complex form, which is easier if you know the animal's anatomy. In order to show the muscle structure, this image shows an exaggerated example of a lion's front leg and paw.

SMOOTH

For very short fur or smooth skin, add graphite evenly. Blend with a cotton swab, blending stump, or piece of tissue if needed.

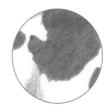

SCALY

For scaly animals like reptiles or dragons, create each individual scale with a tiny arc. Then add shadows to make the form look three-dimensional.

For a much easier way to get a scaly look, just add a bunch of squiggles! Make the squiggles darker in areas of pattern, as well as when adding shadows.

FEATHERED When adding texture to feathered animals, approach it as you would with fur or with smooth skin. Use a series of short strokes for fine or fluffy feathers. For smooth feathers, use even, blended value.

JAGUAR

1

Lightly draw a big circle as a guide for the jaguar's head. Then draw two curved lines across the circle as guides to help you place the facial features later.

2

Add two arcs on top of the head for ears and another circle to help you draw the muzzle.

3

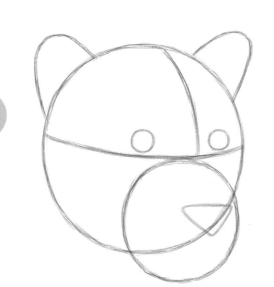

Now draw two small circles as guides for the eyes and a triangle for the nose.

4

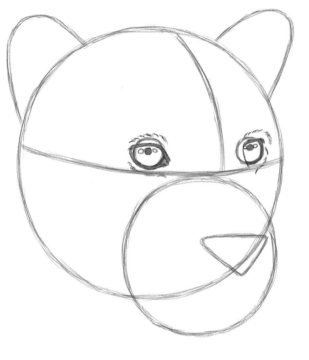

Begin with the eyes, taking your time and sketching lightly at first. The big cat's head is slightly turned, so the eye on the right should be a bit smaller than the eye on the left. Add the details in and around the eye, including some fur around the eyes with quick, short pencil strokes.

5

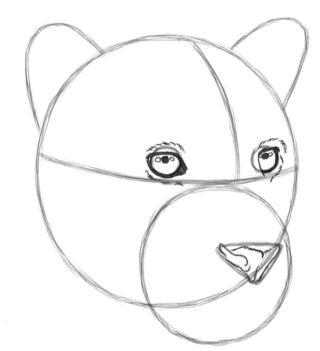

Use the triangle inside the muzzle as a guide to draw the nose. Follow the basic path of the guide, but make the top edge wavier. Note that one of the nostrils isn't visible because the head is turned.

Now lightly sketch the jaguar's muzzle. Use the reference to see where the lines should be smooth or where they should have the furry texture created with short pencil strokes.

Darken the arcs on top of the head for the ears. Extend the lines down into the head circle. Then add a series of pencil strokes for the fur found inside.

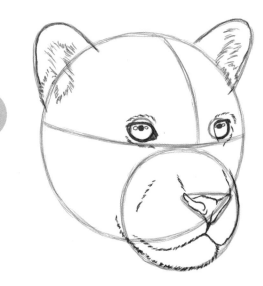

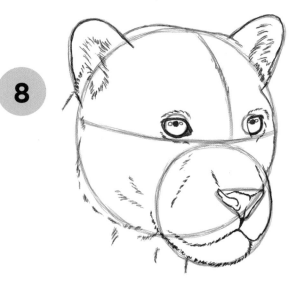

Use the big circle as a guide to draw the head. Note the head lines in relation to the original circle, where they should be drawn inside and outside of the circle, and where they are smooth and when they are made of short strokes. Add some additional detail lines in the face and neck area.

9

For a cleaner look, erase as much as you can of the initial guide lines. Don't worry about erasing all of the guides. It's OK to leave some behind. Re-draw any final sketch lines you may have accidentally erased.

10

Jaguars don't have perfectly circular spots, so just draw circle-like shapes and fill them in with a dark value. Make the markings small near the middle of the head and big near the outside. Shade the nose with a medium value, and use a dark value for the nostril and inside the ears. Use a light-to-medium value to shade the rest of the head. Leave areas around the eyes, ears, muzzle, and lower jaw white, but add a bit of light value there for some shadows. Finally, add some long strokes for whiskers.

SHADING Black panthers are melanistic variations of jaguars and leopards, so you can use black value all over your drawing for a black panther. If you decide to add spots, remember that shading can take a very long time to complete, so be patient and take breaks. Slowly build up the value by adding strokes until you're happy with the result, and make sure to use pencil strokes that go in the general direction of the fur. Also separate each individual stroke a bit so that the white of the paper comes through, which creates a fur-like texture.

1

Draw three circles for the kangaroo's head and body. Note their sizes and placement.

2

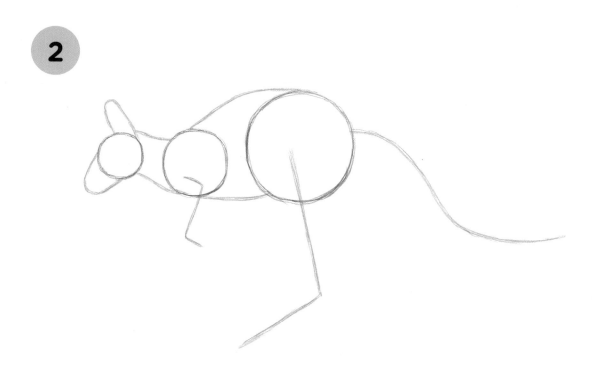

Add arcs for the muzzle and ears, and lines for the legs, tail, and the rest of the body. Now you have all of the guide lines you need to draw a hopping kangaroo!

3

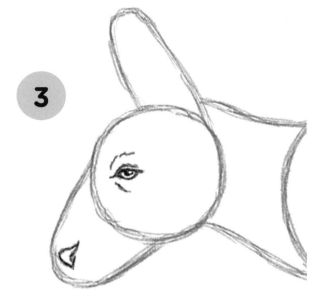

Lightly sketch the eye and nose, and darken the lines when you are happy with them. Shade the pupil and add tiny circle off to the side to represent highlights. Add details around the eye, including the eyelid and eyebrow.

4

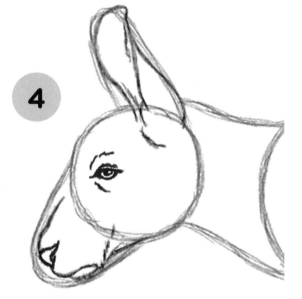

Now draw the muzzle and ear, paying close attention to all of the lines in the image.

5

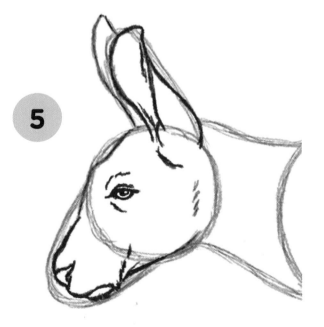

Finish up the kangaroo's head, including the visible portion of the other ear.

Sketch the shape of the arm around the guide. The top part should be wide, and after the bend, it should get thinner. Curve the bottom part to the right and add the small digits and claws.

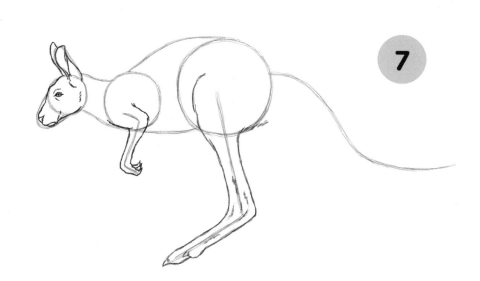

6

Now use the long, angled line on the right as a guide to sketch in the hind leg. Notice how big this leg is in relation to the rest of the body. When you get the shape right, darken the lines. Draw two toes and claws, and add a few short strokes inside the leg for the fur and the outline of the tendons.

7

Because we are viewing the kangaroo from the side, only a very small portion of the limbs on the other side are visible. Draw these, as well as the rest of the body. Simply darken the outer edges of the guide and add some shaggy fur on the bottom. The tail should have a thick base and a thin tip.

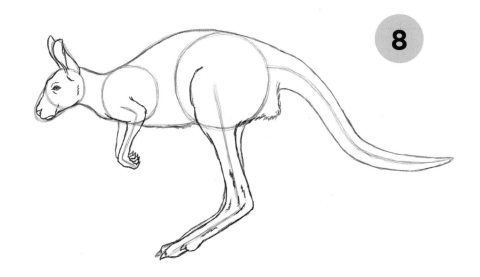

8

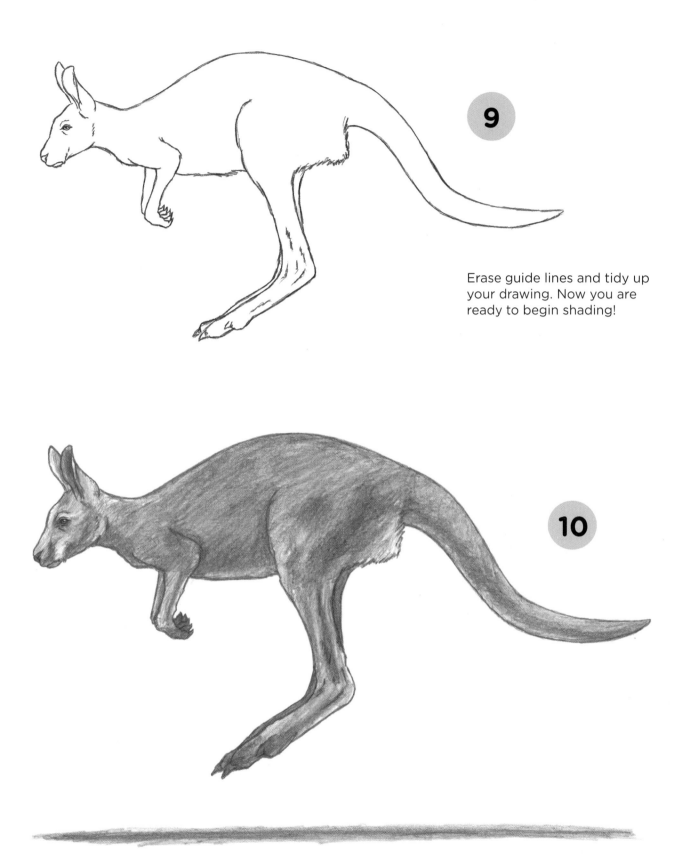

9

Erase guide lines and tidy up your drawing. Now you are ready to begin shading!

10

Add some shading to your drawing to give it more dimension and volume. Add a cast shadow underneath to show that the kangaroo is jumping. The lower the shadow, the higher off the ground the kangaroo will be. Then use a medium value throughout the body. Darken up the shadows as you shade. The toes and fingers should be darker too.

WOLF

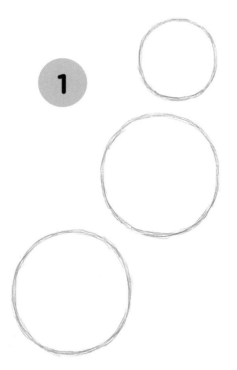

1 Draw three circles for the body and head. Note their sizes and placements.

Create a couple of arcs on top of the head as guides for the muzzle. Add another small arc on the left side of the head as a guide for the ears. Draw two lines under the body as guides for the legs.

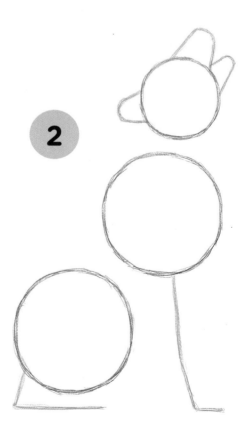

2

3

Draw a few lines that connect the major shapes and form the body. Then add a long, curved line on the lower, left side as a guide for the tail.

4

Draw a short, thick line for the closed eye and add a few smaller lines around it for extra detail. Draw the nose on the tip of the muzzle and shade it in, making the nostril the darkest part. Then use the arc on the left to create the ears. Use quick, short pencil strokes for the fur inside the ear.

5

Add the rest of the head and muzzle, following the initial guide lines. Thick lines make up the lips, and two small triangles make the canine teeth.

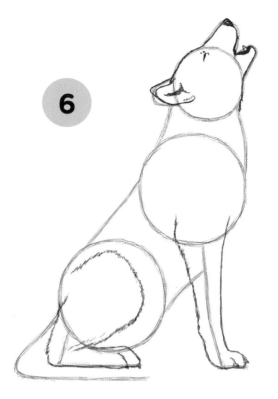

6

Lightly sketch the shapes of the first two legs as you follow the guides. Bend the legs at the joints and add some lines at the bottom for the toes and nails.

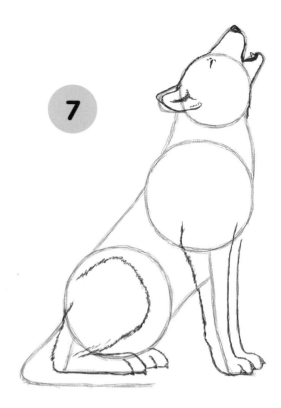

7

Draw the visible portions of the other legs using the first legs as a template.

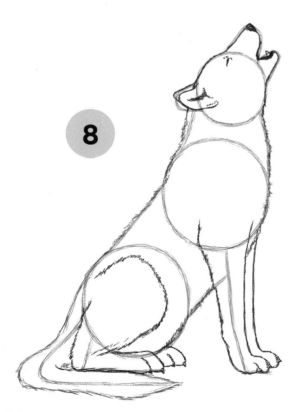

8

Draw the rest of the body and tail by using quick, short strokes to represent the wolf's thick coat as you follow the basic path of the guides.

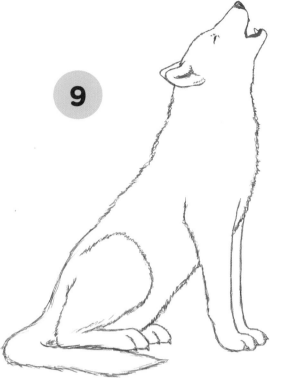

9

Either leave your drawing as a sketch or, for a cleaner look, erase as much as you can of the initial guide lines and tidy up your drawing.

TEXTURE With furry animals, don't worry about shading too smoothly. A rough value will give the coat a coarse fur texture. Just remember to use strokes that go in the direction that the fur grows.

10

For a white wolf or an arctic wolf, just add shadows to give it some dimension and volume. Also add a cast shadow underneath so it looks like it's sitting on the ground. For a gray wolf like this one, keep adding value.

CHIMPANZEE

Draw three circles as guides for the body and head. Under the head circle, draw an arc similar to the letter U for the jaw and chin.

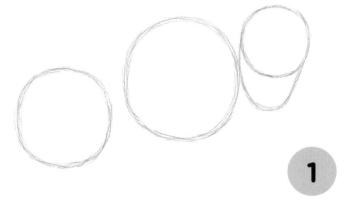

1

Draw two intersecting lines inside the entire head shape, which will help you draw the facial features later on. Add a small C shape for the ear, and then connect the major shapes to form the body.

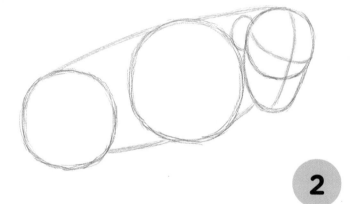

2

Sketch in lines and oval-like shapes for the limbs.

3

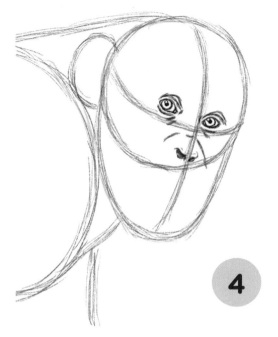

Draw the eyes using the lines as guides for placement. Add a few lines around the eye for wrinkles. Then draw two nostrils and a few lines around them for the outer nose structure.

EYES When drawing many animals' eyes, add a tiny circle off to the side for the highlight. In the middle of the eye, draw a slightly bigger circle for the pupil. Shade the pupil using a dark value.

4

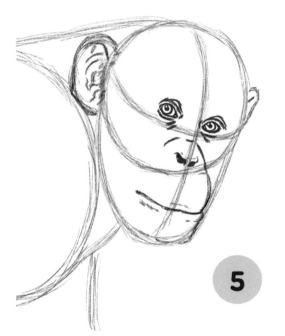

5

Draw the mouth as a horizontal line and some smaller lines to suggest the lips. Connect the right side of the mouth with the nose and add lines under the mouth for the chin. Then draw the ear, adding a few lines inside the shape for the inner structure. Draw a small arc on the right side of the head for the ear on the other side.

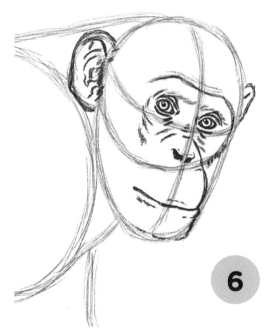

6

Draw a few more lines inside the face for extra detail, including small lines for more wrinkles and a line above the eyes for the thick brow.

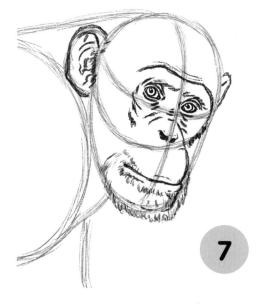

7

Finish the bottom part of the face using quick, short, vertical pencil strokes.

8

Complete the head with the same kind of strokes for a hairy look.

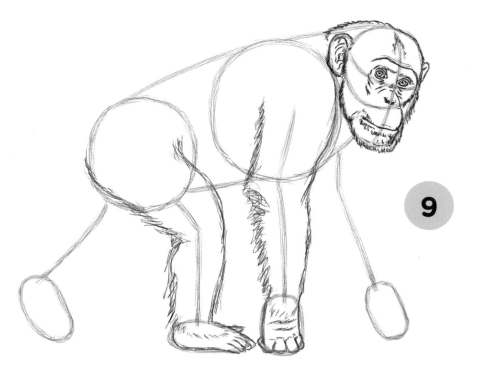

9

Use the two lines in the middle to draw one leg and one arm. Follow the path of the line using quick, short strokes for the hair. Bend the shapes at the knee and elbow. Use the oval-like shapes at the bottom as a guide to draw the foot and hand. Chimps walk on their knuckles, so draw the bent fingers with curved lines. Draw some lines in the hands for detail.

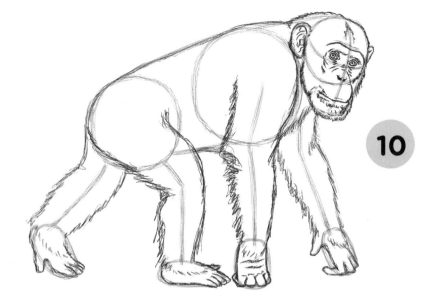

10 Finish the body shape with smooth lines, but add longer hair to the chest. Draw the leg and arm on the other side the same way that you did the first leg and arm. Draw the opposable toe and the toes at the tip. On the hand, draw the thumb near the top and curved lines for the folded fingers at the bottom.

11 Clean up your drawing and get ready to add the shading.

12 As you shade, use pencil strokes that go in the direction of the hair growth. First add the shadows, and then go back through to add a medium value throughout.

LION

Lightly sketch three circles as guides for the lion's head and body. Pay attention to the sizes and placement of the circles in relation to one another.

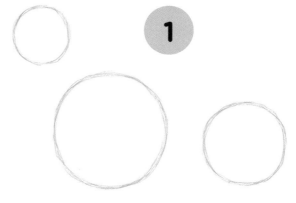

On the head, add guides for the open roaring mouth and an arc for the ear. Then draw four angled lines for the legs and feet.

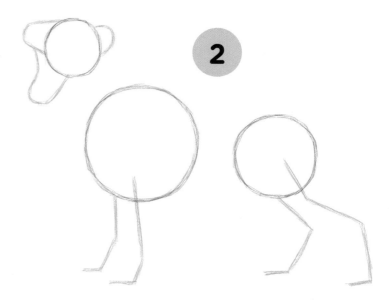

Finish up your guide lines for the body and tail.

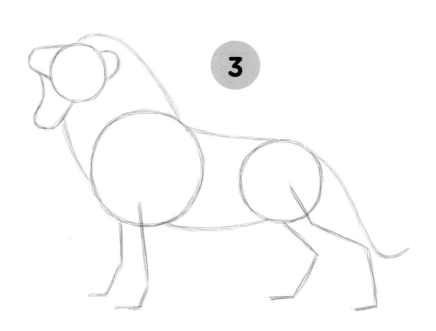

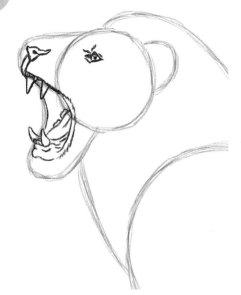

A line similar to a greater-than sign (>) starts the eye. Close off the shape with a short, curved line; add a dot for the pupil; and draw wrinkles around the eye. Draw the nose with straight and wavy lines, and then start on the open mouth, which has two large canines and some smaller teeth.

Pay attention to all the details in the mouth, including the lips, tongue, teeth, and gums.

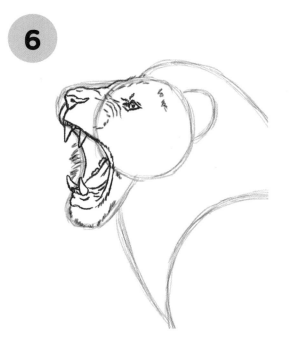

Finish up the chin with quick, short pencil strokes, and add some longer strokes to the left of the mouth to represent some of the long mane. Darken the line above the nose to create the muzzle and add some short lines between the nose and the eyes for wrinkles.

Darken the ear guide and add some short strokes inside the shape for fur. Then use quick strokes for the front part of the lion's mane.

Use the guides to draw the first two legs. Add a couple of curved lines inside of the paw for the toes, as well as tiny claws. At the top of the front leg, draw a tuft of fur. Also add some detail lines.

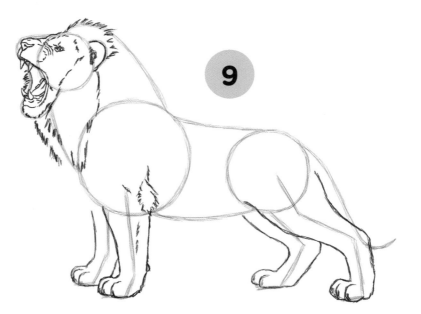

Now draw the other two legs. Don't forget to add the toes and claws on the paws.

Complete the mane using longer pencil strokes to indicate the long fur. Then darken the guides to finish the body. Draw the tail and add a tuft of fur at the end.

11

Clean up your drawing by erasing guide lines, and re-draw anything you'd like before moving on to shading.

12

Shade your lion, keeping in mind that areas around the mouth are the lightest parts of the drawing and the inside the mouth and parts of the tufts of fur are the darkest. The body is a light-to-medium value, with some shadows to add volume and structure. Don't forget to add the cast shadow under your lion!

ALLIGATOR

Lightly sketch three circles as guides for the alligator's head and body. Remember, you don't need to make your circles perfect, but do pay attention to the placement of the circles.

1

Draw two long arcs on the left side of the head as guides for the open mouth. Then connect the major shapes to form the alligator's body.

2

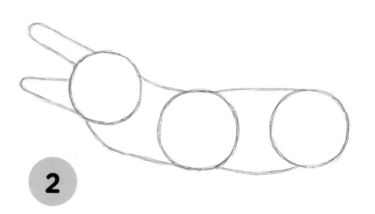

Sketch three angled lines under the body for the short legs. Bend them to indicate where the joints will be. Then draw two long, curved lines for the tail.

3

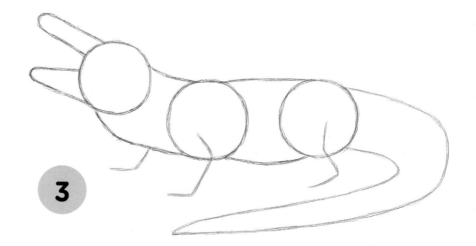

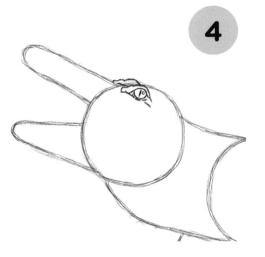

4

Draw the eye as a small circle near the top of the head circle. Add a slit pupil and a circle for the highlight. Draw the brow over the eye and the visible portion of the brow on the other side of the head. Add a few lines under the eye as well for extra detail.

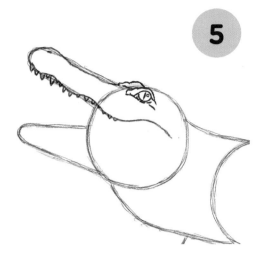

5

Using the top arc, draw the top snout, making the line bumpier at the top and wavier at the bottom. The bottom should stretch far to the right. Once you get the shape of the snout right, add a series of small, different-sized triangle shapes for the teeth.

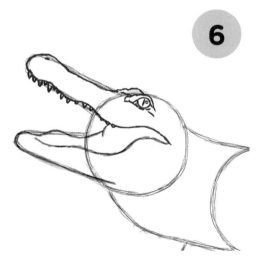

6

Now add the bottom jaw. The top should be wavy and the bottom part straight.

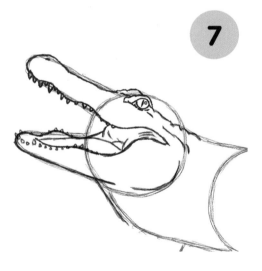

7

Add the sharp teeth, the tongue, and additional details inside of the throat. Then complete the rest of the alligator's head and neck. Make the top part of the head bumpy and the bottom smooth. Add a curved line on the right for the powerful jaw.

Draw the legs that are on this side of the body with smooth, curved lines. Add details on the digits and where the legs connect to the body.

8

Add the spikes on the back and tail. Note that where the tail curves, there is a second row of spikes.

9

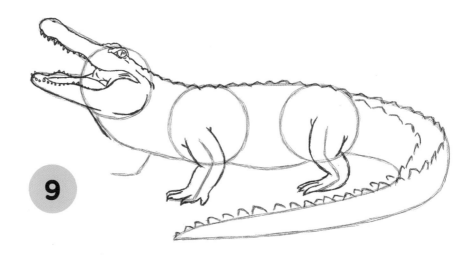

Finish up the bottom part of the body and lines on the tail, and then add the other front leg. The other hind leg is not visible from this angle.

10

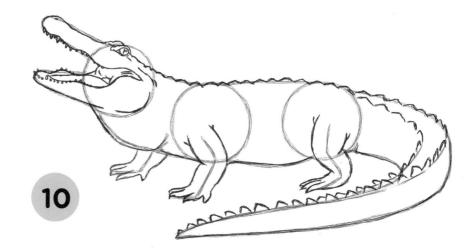

11

Tidy up your sketch and erase any visible guide lines.

12

Add value for more detail, keeping the light source in mind so your shadows are consistent. To get a rough texture, use random scribbles instead of smooth shading. The top part of an alligator tends to be darker, while the underside is usually lighter. The bottom part is also less bumpy, so don't add the squiggles there. Instead, draw grid-like lines for the scales.

CAST SHADOWS An animal will create a cast shadow when it blocks light from hitting the ground. Adding this shadow to your drawing will make it look like the animal is on the ground, rather than floating in the air. When adding a large cast shadow like this one, make sure to use a darker value near the middle of the shadow and a lighter value along the edge. The darkest places are where less light is able to reach.

GRIZZLY BEAR

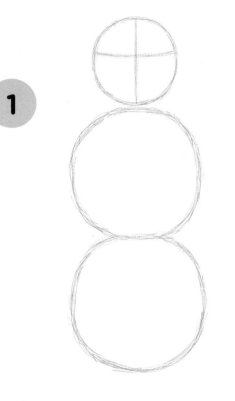

1

First lightly sketch three circles on top of each other. Then add two intersecting lines inside the top circle, which will help you place the facial features later on.

2

Add guides for the ears, muzzle, and limbs using arcs, circles, and lines.

3

Draw the small eyes using the lines as guides for placement, and add a few lines around them for extra detail. Use quick, short strokes to draw the furry brow. Then look carefully at the nose in this image and try to replicate it on your paper.

Complete the rest of the muzzle with quick, short strokes for the furry texture. Don't forget the lip and chin. Then use the arcs on the head as guides to draw the ears. Also use quick, short strokes here for the furry texture, and add more strokes within the ear shape for the fuzzy inner ear.

4

5

Again using quick, short strokes for fur, use the original circle as a guide to draw the rest of the head and neck.

6

Draw the shoulders, front legs, and paws. The digits on the paws are tiny lines at the bottom of the ovals. Then draw even smaller lines at the end for the claws.

7

Use the lines at the bottom as guides for the hind legs. Make the lines look furry, and add the toes and claws at the end.

8

Draw the bear's stomach with quick, short strokes, and add a few extra furry lines inside for more detail.

9

Tidy up your sketch by erasing guide lines and re-drawing anything you'd like to fix.

10

Add some shading to your grizzly bear drawing to give it more dimension and volume. Pick the direction of the light source when shading so that the shadows are consistent. Also add a cast shadow underneath the bear so it doesn't appear to be floating. Then add more value using strokes with a vertical orientation to suggest how the fur hangs down.

AFRICAN ELEPHANT

1

For the body and head guides, draw two circles and a large arc coming off the circle on the right.

2

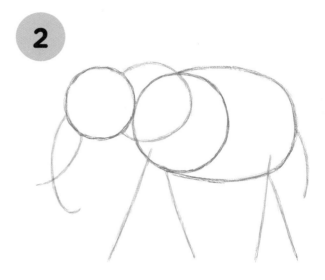

Add a large arc for the ear and some straight and curved lines for the trunk, tusks, legs, and tail.

3

The eye is just a half circle with another shaded half circle inside for the pupil. Elephants are wrinkly, so draw a few lines around the eye to represent this.

4

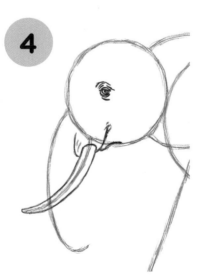

Use the guide line to draw the elephant's tusk and mouth. Simply thicken the line and end it at a point. Draw the folds of skin at the base of it and the bottom lip next to it.

5

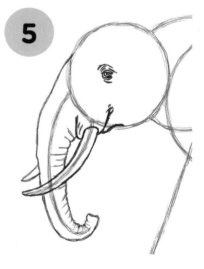

The trunk shouldn't be smooth. Draw a few lines on it to represent the folds and wrinkles. Add the tip of the tusk that's hiding behind the trunk too.

6

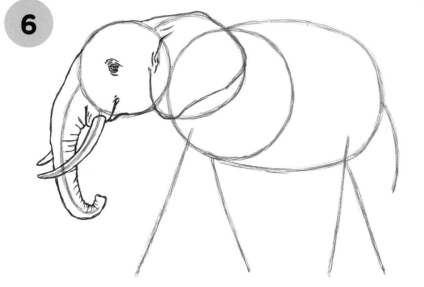

This is an African elephant, so draw a big ear and make it angled. Include a few lines at the base of it for the inner structure. Then finish the head using the remaining guides.

7

Draw all around the leg guide using bumpy lines. Elephants have wide feet, so make the bottom part bulge out and draw a few arcs for the nails. Add some wrinkles at the joint.

8

Draw the hind leg the same way.

9

You'll come back to the feet in the next step. Now complete the elephant's body, making the lines curve and bend throughout. Also draw the tail, including the brushy part at the end of it.

10

Now that you've drawn the stomach, you can finish up the legs on the other side of the body using the first legs as templates.

11

DIMENSION & VOLUME
To create realistic shadows that make a drawing look three-dimensional, keep in mind where the light source is coming from. Then add the shadows where they would fall in real life. It takes time and practice to learn this skill, so as you're learning, pay close attention to your references (in this case, the final step). Copy what you see, taking note where light source could be and where the shadows fall.

For a cleaner look, erase as much as you can of the initial guide lines. Don't worry about erasing all the guides. It's OK to leave some behind and re-draw any lines that you accidentally erase.

12

Add shading to give your elephant drawing more volume and dimension, and add a cast shadow so it doesn't appear to be floating. Elephants are wrinkly, so draw some extra lines all over. Because they are gray, add value throughout the body, creating areas of light and dark where light and shadows fall.

39

TIGER

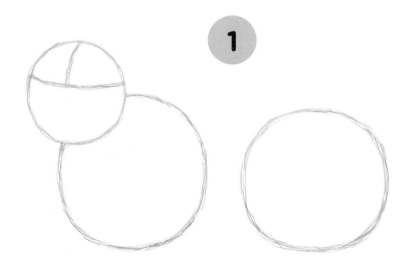

Draw two circles as guides for the body and a circle for the head. Add two curved lines in the head to help you place the tiger's facial features later on.

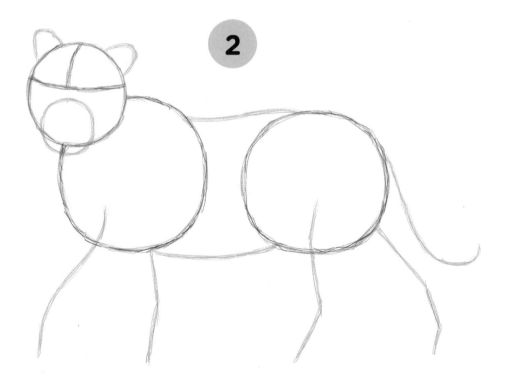

Connect the body circles. Then draw two small arcs for ears on top of the head, a circle for the muzzle, lines for the legs, and a line for the tail.

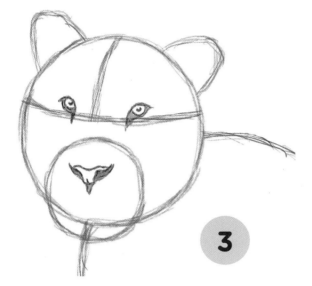

The eyes are shaped like footballs with two circles inside each for the eyeball and pupil. Surround the eyes with a darker outline that comes to a point underneath. The nose resembles an upside-down triangle with shaded sides for the nostrils.

3

Draw a line below the nose that splits and curves up on both sides. Then add the lower jaw as a shaded shape with a curved line under it for the chin.

4

Use quick, short strokes to create the furry face shape. Darken the ear arcs and add fur inside.

5

Draw the first two legs using the initial lines as guides, adding furry areas at the top and toes on the paws. Draw lightly at first. When you like what you have, go ahead and darken it.

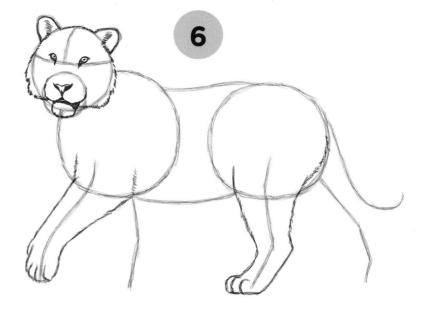

Draw the other legs the same way. Surround the line by sketching lightly at first. Then darken it using quick, short strokes.

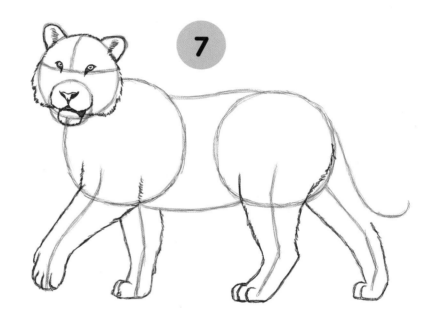

Finish up the body and add the tail.

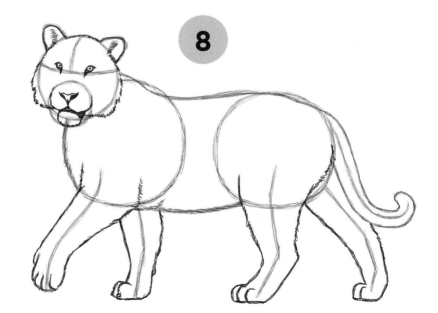

9

Erase your guide lines and get ready to add the tiger's striped coat pattern!

10

To draw the stripes, sketch pointy shapes and shade them in. The stripes should wrap around the body, so keep the overall body shape in mind as you draw the stripes. Use this image as a reference for accuracy in the placement of the stripes, or have fun and draw them where you want! Once you're done with the stripes, add some shading to give your tiger drawing more dimension and volume, and don't forget the cast shadow underneath. Add a medium value where the orange color appears on the coat, and leave the white areas very lightly shaded or completely blank.

GIRAFFE

For the head, neck, and body guides, lightly sketch three circles and some lines to connect them.

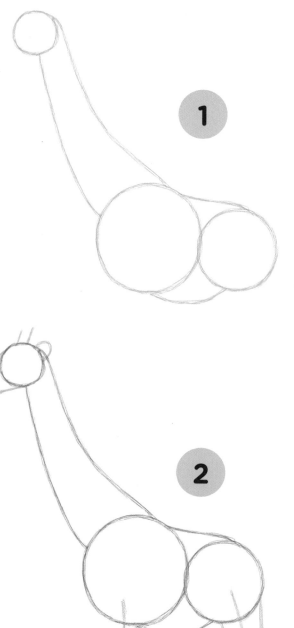

1

Finish your initial sketch with guides for horns, an ear, the muzzle, the legs, and the tail.

2

GUIDE LINES For the first few steps, don't press down too hard with your pencil. Use light, smooth strokes to begin so that it's easy to erase if you make a mistake and want to re-draw something that wasn't quite right. Also don't worry if your circles aren't perfect. Turn back to page 5 to refresh your memory on how to draw a circle. You will erase guide lines later on, so instead of worrying about making a perfect circle, focus more on its size and placement in relation to the rest of the shapes.

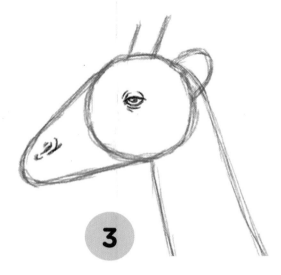

Draw the half-shut eye and add some lines around the eye for detail. Then draw a nostril near the tip of the muzzle guide and add a few curved lines around the nostril to give the nose more structure.

3

Use wavy lines for the top of the muzzle above the nose, mouth, lower lip, and chin. Use the small arc on the head to draw the ear, which has a lot of curved lines within the shape to give it more structure. Then draw the horns, which look like cylinders with furry tops.

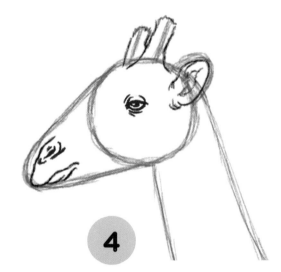

4

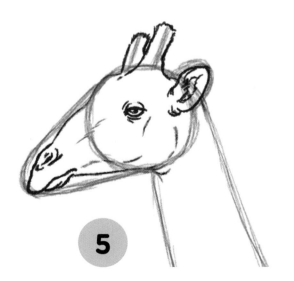

5

Without overlapping the horns or ears, draw the rest of the head with wavy lines. The bottom part of the head should be narrower than the arc. Add a few short lines inside the head to emphasize its structure.

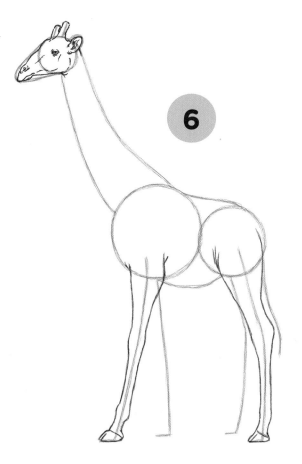

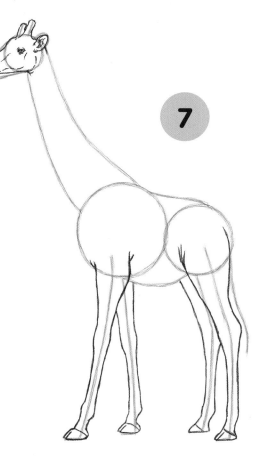

Draw the long, thin legs that are on this side of the body using wavy lines that bulge at the joints. Add the hooves at the bottom, with a line in the middle to split them in two.

Draw the visible portions of the other two legs the same way.

Darken the neck, adding a hump at the bottom of the right side. Along the right edge, add the short mane. Finish the rest of the body by darkening the outer edges of the initial guides. Then add the tail, including a series of long, wavy lines at the tip for the hair found there.

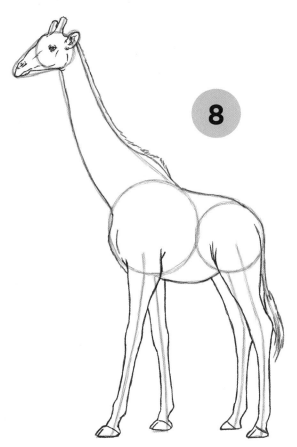

Erase any lines you don't want to keep and finalize the lines you do want.

9

10

Add shadows to your giraffe, and add a cast shadow. With a medium value, add the spots on the body, which fade on the legs. Darker areas include the nostril, eyes, tips of the horns, inner ear, mane, tail, and hooves.

ABOUT THE AUTHOR

How2DrawAnimals.com teaches beginning artists how to draw all kinds of animals from A to Z through video demonstrations and simple step-by-step instructions. Started in 2012 by an animal-loving artist with a bachelor's degree in illustration, How2DrawAnimals offers a new tutorial each week and now boasts hundreds of animal drawing tutorials. Working in graphite and in colored pencils, and in both realistic and cartoon styles, How2DrawAnimals has featured animals from all letters of the alphabet, from Aardvark to Zebra and everything in between. See more at How2DrawAnimals.com.

ALSO IN THE LET'S DRAW SERIES:

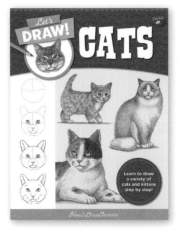

Let's Draw Cats
ISBN: 978-0-7603-8070-3

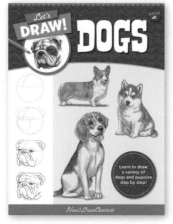

Let's Draw Dogs
ISBN: 978-0-7603-8072-7

Let's Draw Favorite Animals
ISBN: 978-0-7603-8074-1

Let's Draw Birds & Butterflies
ISBN: 978-0-7603-8078-9

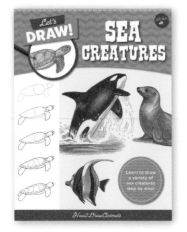

Let's Draw Sea Creatures
ISBN: 978-0-7603-8080-2

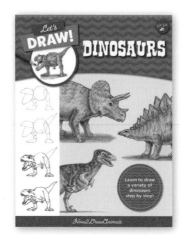

Let's Draw Dinosaurs
ISBN: 978-0-7603-8082-6

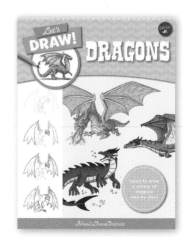

Let's Draw Dragons
ISBN: 978-0-7603-8084-0

The Quarto Group

Inspiring | Educating | Creating | Entertaining

www.WalterFoster.com

Walter Foster Jr.